Published by Swan Press,
32 Joy Street,
Dublin 4

© Swan Press and author, 1999

ISBN   0 9521342 7 6

Front Cover: Design by Maura O'Grady based on photograph by
Mary Guckian of Creel made by Patrick Guckian.

Layout: Gillian Gray

Back Cover: Photograph by Paul Wearen

Inside: Photographs by Mary Guckian

Set by M Shine, Dublin.

CONTENTS

Acknowledgements

Some of the poems in this collection have appeared previously in the following publications: *Extended Wings I, Quartet, Aisling, Asylum, Acorn 5, Books Ireland, Force 10, Mayo Anthology, Reality, Riposte, Studies, Women's Work VI, VII, VIII, Leitrim Guardian, Brobdingnagian Times, Cahoots, Cerberus* (USA), *BrouHaha* (USA), *Exile, Lateral Moves, Reflections, Rustic Rub, T.O.P.S, Labour of Love (Canada), Poetry Now, Hear My Song, Perceptions, Peer Poetry, ZZ Zyne* (USA) *Interpreter's House, Deireadh Re - Carrick-on-Shannon Vocational School 1932-1994, Leitrim Observer* (Centenary Publication).

Some poems were also broadcast on radio: Anna Livia, RTE, Dublin City University.

I would like to thank the members of the Rathmines Writers' Workshop for their great support over the years and Mary Shine for her editorial assistance during the production of this anthology.

I am also very grateful to Mary O'Donnell for her invaluable assistance and encouragement.

Dedicated to my father, Patrick, who believed that
'if a job is worth doing it is worth doing well.'
He was born at the beginning of this century and left
a legacy of work in the creels, armchairs and
farm tools that he made. He built the house where
I was born, and it grew from a three roomed thatched
cottage to a large farmhouse. He died in 1970.

IRONING

Years of ironing starched shirt collars
for my father and the aprons
we wore for cookery class in school,
gave a polished surface to the clothes iron.

The end opened like the lid of a box
and out came the large stone which
we buried in the centre of the open fire,
until it turned pink-red, like a slab of jelly.

With the tongs we lifted the stone
from the fire, transferred it to the iron
and began ironing the clothes.
As we moved it over and back

on the garments, the creases vanished.
Every fifteen minutes we placed the stone
back in the fire, until clothes for seven of us
were neatly ironed and stacked,

ready for another week

CREELS

My father spent hours
trimming the edges
of the newly cut sally rods,
to make creels for taking the turf
over the soft soil of the bog,
so that the horse and cart
could bring it home
for the winter time.
I watched how he scalloped
the edges, tightly tied
and intricately weaved
the freshwood.

He was always making tools,
repairing them.
Busy with his hands,
he wasted no time,
took no holidays,
or trips away, except once
a year, cycling to Mohill
for the Manachan Day Fair
with my mother.
When they got home,
the sun was a low ember,
the cows milked.

PICKING POTATOES AFTER SCHOOL

During October and November,
after the bitter four mile cycle
from the school,
I'd eat my dinner,
then face the job of picking potatoes
from the long ridges
my father had dug with a spade,
in one of the fields during the day.

The bigger spuds were put in clamps
in the field, neatly covered with clay
for the winter,
to keep away birds and mice.
Sometimes, my sisters had picked them,
leaving the poicíns for me,
to be boiled later for pigs and hens,
in the great pot on the open fire.

Old Creamery Can at Kiltoghert.

Photograph taken by Mary Guckian

CHURNING THE MILK, 1949.

Every Monday after school
churning had to be done.
Milk that went sour on Sunday
was turned into butter on Monday,
as the creamery was closed
on the seventh day of the week.

Sometimes we kept it fresh
by putting the can into the pool,
where we buried it half way up
to the handles.

It was heavy, even when empty.
When milk went sour we churned
with a heavy wooden handle,
inserted into the can,
shaped like a cross.

We sealed it with a wooden lid,
fitted over the churn,
moving it up and down,
splashing the milk into a thick
butter that floated to the top.

Afterwards we drank mugfuls
of buttermilk to quench our thirst.

PREPARING FOR THE STATION

During March and October
Mass was celebrated in each
       townland;
much painting and cleaning
took up the time beforehand.
Each piece of wood had to be
       prepared;
poor chimney draughts
made the drying of paint difficult.
Everyone worried
that the neighbours might get
their clothes ruined,
or that the priest's wide cloak
might blow against the door post.
China dishes were washed and
       scoured.
Old white tablecloths
       with silvery designs
were washed and starched;
the ironing brought up the
       pattern.
The towels edged with heavy
       lace
were used for the small tables,
where the priest laid his particles
before saying Mass.

Bedspreads never seen before
came out of old trunks,
the Sacred Heart Lamp was
        polished
along with brass candlesticks.
The priest gave a sermon
telling us to love our neighbour.
If a family from the townland
        was missing
it was assumed a row was
        brewing,
or it could be that they wanted
to avoid the next turn for Mass.
The priest never left
without a volunteer promising
to take the next Station.
Lots of food was served
for breakfast in the parlour.

THE MASTER'S BICYCLE

A second hand bicycle
was all the master could afford,
when he came to teach
in our country school.
After years of cycling
the four miles in the rain,
it disjointed.
The saddle sat loosely,
padded with papers and rags.
During lunch hour the boys
loved to pull it apart,
leaving the saddle at an angle
that made a pyramid
of the well-worn seat.
It was all they could to do
to get back at him, as he
lashed their growing hands
with the sally rod.

THE TRAVELLERS' TENT

Down at the cross-roads on my way to school,
I would cycle past the travellers
and watch the steam rise
from the dark brown dusky tent.
Shaped like the last quarter of the moon,
it was tiny,
a family lived here quietly
mending our buckets,
making pongers
in different sizes.

We exchanged vegetables and milk
for the goods they provided
tin pongers, buckets
and crepe paper flowers.

After nights of heavy rain
they woke to find
the sagging canvas
sink into the tiny space,
their only heat
the closely packed bodies
within the small tent.

WORKING AT THE RATE BOOKS

I climbed the steps to the Courthouse,
entered the large stone building; the sound
of my footsteps echoed through the space.

A stone stairs led me to the Council Chamber,
a room covered in wood, where numerous
Council meetings must have taken place.

The eerie smell of history lingered in the room
as six of us wrote out the rates for the whole county.
We entered figures on the many columned pages
of the Rates Inspector's large, well-bound books.

At one o clock each day I dined at Prior's.
The four course lunch renewed my energy,
and two months later all the work was done.

FAIR DAY AT CARRICK

Jostling between the cattle
as they crowded the street
with steaming bodies,
I steered my bicycle to school.

Fresh manure lay
in puddles on the ground,
plastering my shoes
with sloppy mush.

Men with caps and hats
at all angles, slapped hands
and bargained, buying
and selling all day long.

Many shop windows
were nailed with slats of wood,
to prevent the glass
being gored by horns.

A few livelier beasts might
wander into pubs and shops,
causing consternation.

On my way home,
shopkeepers with buckets
of water and yardbrushes,
tried to clean the street,

but it still reeked of beasts
and a day of dung.

HARNESSING THE HORSE

The ritual took place
on the street outside my home,
during most of our childhood.
Before tackling the horse
to bring milk to the creamery,
my father went to the field
with a rope loosely made
in the shape of a bridle.

Speaking gently to Captain,
he would throw the loop
around his neck, swinging
it firmly on his face.
Coloured chestnut and white,
we patted him softly, as my father
carried each piece of harness
from the cart house nearby.

The brass shone in the sunshine.
Even on dark misty days
the large buckles glowed, .
that held each piece together.
The winkers were heavy across Captain's ears
buckling around his long face,
the bit pushing into his mouth.
He shook his head
aiming to break free.

The collar placed around
his neck was firmly shaped,
well padded with horse shavings;

it lay heavily on the wiry hair
that hung from his neck,
the hams looked awkward
when they fell apart,
but they sat comfortably
into the ridges of the collar.

The heavy weight of the saddle
was raised onto his back,
a band placed under his body
and buckled to the other side.
As children we went under
his feet to catch the belt
and take it underneath the body.
My mother might see us and shout
'Keep away from the horse.'

The brichen, the last piece,
slid onto his rounded flanks
pulling the tail across the band,
making him comfortable;
he was now ready to be eased under
the shafts of the cart,
pointing towards the sky,
my father coaxing him gently,
'back-up, back-up.'

With a crash the chain fell
heavily across the saddle,
the belly band was tied underneath
the shafts and hams made secure,
and Captain was anxious to be off.
We listened to the heavy sound
of the cart wheel going out the lane,
heading for Kiltoghert Co-Op.

HOMEBOY

Taken from his mother at birth
and reared in the County Home,
left with strangers on a farm at fourteen,
there was no time for education.

A life of slavery lay before him,
working for abusive farming men
and women.
He grew old in his youth,
suffering backache from hard work
and wettings as he laboured
at every job he was given.
Sleeping in lofts, cattle gave heat
to his tired body night after night.

The farmers he had slaved for
know nothing of his whereabouts.
In his sixties, on a week's holiday
paid for by the St. Vincent De Paul,
he enjoys the company of women,
and is overcome
when given a present of a book,
or a woman asks for his address.

Never before getting as much
as a Christmas card,
this old man seems cared for,
happy in Knock.

THE EGGLER

Jimmy Reilly, the eggler, sat in a comfortable seat, like a king on his throne, in the middle of the neatly packed boxes as he drove his horse and cart from the local town, arriving in our townland every Thursday. A white-haired man in a raincoat, he steered the heavy load of groceries and the boxes he used for collecting the eggs, up the hills and down the hollows of the pot holed country roads.

He brought us the Irish Press, the only daily paper purchased during the week and we read it from beginning to end, trying to grasp the stories with foreign place names and learn about the big world that seemed so distant to us then. We had no radio to interrupt our childish vision and we had little time to read but the fashion photos excited my eyes. On wet days we spent the hours indoors cutting out pictures of hats that looked like up-turned flower pots and skirts that were pencil slim over smooth legs that wore stockings with seams and spiky heeled shoes. Admiring these designs I pasted them neatly into my old school copy-books from time to time.

The eggs were collected during the week from nests in the henhouse by us children, where we regularly placed golden straw or fresh smelling hay and made the nests cosy for the hens to lie down and wait to lay their eggs. Some of the hens preferred open spaces and we might find the warm eggs in ditches or in part of the hayshed and ran home excitedly carrying them in our up-turned skirts.

My mother, after they were cleaned, gave them to the eggler in exchange for goods needed for the week for our family. Prices varied and the big worry was always "what price are the eggs today?" The price went down the more we had and up if they were scarce. I looked forward to the juicy tomatoes for tea that evening with the large plain loaves of bread. Empty packets of jelly and custard were used for playing shop under the big sycamore tree at the top of the garden. We kept an eye out for new boxes to add to our stock. Sometimes salt with Lot's wife would be among the groceries my mother bought, along with packets of green peas, Indian tea and sugar.

The caraway seed cake was a special treat but it was often sold out by the time the eggler travelled the four miles to our house from the local town.

On frosty days the horse had to be led sideways up and down the steep hills and when the roads were slippy or full of snow Jimmy never got as far as our house and the number of eggs built up and the bucket got heavy to carry out through the lane.

One time my sister tripped and the eggs got broken and the rich yellow yokes spilled onto the stony path. With tears in our eyes we managed to save some of the eggs and enough were left to buy food for the week.

After all those years, sometimes I hear a whistle in the distance, and a touch of excitement comes over me as I remember the gentle warning that the eggler was on his way. The best memories are of the white horse standing quietly and watching Jimmy finding the groceries among all the boxes in the windings of the maze of his loaded cart.

THREE HAIL MARYS FOR THE CONVERSION OF RUSSIA

We creased the handmade skirts my mother had crafted and made a cushion under our knees on the cement floor. When we knelt for the family rosary around eight o'clock each evening, we took off our shoes and toasted the backs of our toes, as the large ash logs, which my father had cut down to a size that fitted the hearth, sizzled and crackled in the fire.

We faced the altar at the end of the kitchen, made in the appropriate shape from the tiny baby chair, my father had made from old pieces of wood. A narrow piece lay across the arms of the chair and two vases of flowers fresh from the garden were always there. When not available we had paper flowers that the travellers sold us in rich red and turquoise colours.

Statues of Our Lady and St. Joseph were on each side of the pierced Sacred Heart picture given to me at school. The Sacred Heart lamp was always lit, its red glow warmed the kitchen as the darkness came down before we lit the large paraffin lamp. We had to be careful with the oil which came from the local co-op store where we sold our milk; it was entered in number 87 account.

My mother started off the rosary and we held the beads tight in our hands, each having our own in a different colour or maybe another shape. The older children had to say a decade of the rosary but the younger ones only had to say some of the trimmings.

I loved the litany the best - mother most pure, mother most sweet, mother inviolate, mother undefiled, mother most amiable, mirror of justice, seat of wisdom; it went on for ages - these precious new words were only heard at this time and they filled my ears with music.

Then it was on to five Hail Marys for the immortal souls, an act of contrition, three Hail Marys for health and happiness, the long prayer to St. Joseph, more new words - I found them difficult to grasp. I loved the prayer to my Angel Guardian knowing that he always guided me safely past the dark shadows on the wall, as I climbed the stairs to bed, holding the candle tightly to prevent the dancing figures on the wall from jumping out at me.

Three more Hail Marys were said to the Immaculate Conception, three to St. Joseph to preserve us from sudden death, three more to relieve the suffering souls in purgatory, a pater, ave, gloria for all the blessings we received this day and protection for the night, the Hail Holy Queen and near the end, the Memorarae - 'Remember O Most Gracious Virgin Mary.'

As each one of us left home to live elsewhere three Hail Marys were added. I missed out on these being the first to leave. When I returned at week-ends I joined in the privilege of prayers for myself, knowing when we came to the three Hail Marys for Russia, that the rosary was almost over and it was time to raise our bodies from kneeling on the cold cement floor.

AUNTIE NELLIE IN THE NURSING HOME

I am an old woman now of ninety-two, fastened to this seat day after day. I listen for the tick-tock of the grandfather clock, yet all I hear are sounds of people moving, all strangers to me. Remembering my home where I lived all of my life for over fifty years, where John and I watched our eight children weave through all the cycles of life. Now they are scattered across five continents, writing to me regularly. What good are letters. I cannot read any more. All I want is to see one of them, to touch their hands and enjoy the familiarity of someone I know. I long to see the sacred heart lamp burn in front of the picture at the end of the kitchen. For years I filled it with paraffin oil that I bought in the local creamery, trimming the wick often, making sure the flame never died in the delicate globe I polished with my own breathy air.

The nurses here are kind, food is served tastefully, yet all I long for is some of my home-made bread that I baked on the hearth stone for seventy years of my life. If only I could have an open fire, see the red coals and bake an apple tart or a blackberry tart or cook the produce of the season. I see the big pots of potatoes I struggled to lift. I see myself feeding the hens and the pigs the mashed-up potatoes. I see me raking the fire at night, always a spark left to set it alight the next morning. The moaning central heating here is clinical, like the rest of this place. Give me the warmth I crave. Where have all the old photographs gone, the weddings of all my children lined along the walls in the parlour, and of their children at first holy communion. There's nothing in this room only a cold grey crucifix and people I do not know. My mind is full of memories. Please, take me home so that I can be safe in my own territory.

HER FIRST DANCE

At Christmas time Bridgie recalls the hours spent searching for a Christmas card she bought for a man called Andy. She was eighteen years then and had got a lift to the dance at Rooskey on a Sunday night in the month of November. Cloudland Ballroom was one of many with similar titles that sprung up around the countryside during the late fifties and sixties. The name of the hall sounded romantic and caused much excitement as it was Bridgie's first real dance. She dreamed of meeting a gorgeous fellow who would dance with her all night. He would be well dressed, clean, tall and handsome, but she worried she might not be capable of holding an on-going conversation if the need arose. Earlier that day she read the Sunday paper and tried to remember the headlines and hoped she would be able to discuss the politics of the day, the different tragedies, the farmers' prices for cattle and other subjects.

One of the staff from the local creamery gave her and a few local girls a lift, arriving at 10 p.m. The large empty hall had a doorway full of big, strong looking men, one of them standing in an alcove at the side entrance and behind this tiny space he viewed the arrivals. In a tinier space, level with his dark jacket, the money was placed. On the sign, in large, badly written biro, the price said 5/-. Bridgie produced her two half-crowns, while the other girls handed in their cash and the three of them walked towards the cloakroom.

It was full of girls, beautiful and slender, glamorous and intelligent looking, small and delicate, untidy and greasy-haired, queuing to leave in their coats at a cost of 6d. All moved along against a dirty wall, a wall badly in need of paint, leaving their coats with the lady behind the counter. The cracked mirror was grey and misty from the fog of the girls' breaths. All were busy combing their hair, painting their nails and very excited about the night in front of them. Some had boyfriends outside, others hoped that a fellow they admired would be at the dance, some merely wished to get dancing. At this point Bridgie got a bit worried. There were so many girls around, she felt she had little hope of getting a dance. Herself and her pals moved out into the hall finding it big, cold and empty. The band were making all kinds of sounds as they tuned up their equipment. Some of the girls moved towards the front to be nearer the stage and the musicians winked at them and seemed delighted to know they had admirers.

The men were sitting here and there along the sides of the hall, some holding the hands of girls, others standing near the door making slight noises and showing off their tight legged trousers or their newly cut hair. The time passed slowly, the band began to play tunes - 'The Wild Side of Life', 'How much is that Doggie in the Window.' Half way through the tune some of the men got up their courage and asked a few girls to dance. The scene seemed a long journey away from Bridgie's dream. She was getting cold in her light dress. After some time and more couples on the floor a tall gangly fellow danced with her. It was difficult to talk with him as he towered above her and spoke in jerks. He seemed excited to be dancing and was unsure of his words. Bridgie felt worse. All she had rehearsed before the dance left her mind which seemed blank. She muttered about the band playing good tunes and he wondered how often she heard them before.

At the end of the dance he asked her to have a mineral but she was nervous and told him she had to meet her friends. Returning to where she left them she found all had vanished. Standing in an agitated state, not sure where to turn, who to look at, what way to move, she crossed her legs and nearly fell. Folding her arms she moved slightly backwards as the crowds were moving away from the centre of the floor until the next dance commenced. The crowd seemed to be multiplying, with an element of pushing and shoving. Bridgie got nervous. Another fellow caught her arm and dragged her onto the floor. He never said a word until he had her out in the middle of the ballroom. It was a fast number and he tried to swing her to a rock and roll movement. She felt awkward, her feet failed to move with the music, she developed a pain in her arm from the jerking movements he was inflicting on her hand. She asked him to slow down a bit. He opened his mouth and showed a whole plate of loosely fitting false teeth. He was in his mid twenties. She tried to talk to him but could not think of a single thing to say. At the end of the three tunes he ran away without saying a word.

The hall was packed, the air sweaty and smells of aftershave floated around. Brylcream hair oil and the perfume off the girls, mostly apple blossom, and heavy powder seemed to swamp her nostrils. Bridgie looked for an empty seat, finding a tiny space between two couples. Feeling comfortable she decided to sit for the rest of the night. One of the fellows started to chat, leaving the girl beside him to sit and listen. She grew embarrassed having someone else's boyfriend chat her up. She left for the cloakroom finding a sweaty face staring back at her in the mirror. She rubbed the drops of sweat off her brow with the bottom of her light dress. With the wide flowing skirts the stain would not show up. She looked in the mirror again and wondered where all the fellows she dreamed about were hiding.

Bridgie went back into the hall. The entrance to the cloakroom was packed tightly with men and she had to squeeze her way out in order to make a passage to get back to the dance floor. Despite her murmuring 'Excuse me' they all seemed fastened to the floor and unaware of movement around them. When she got as far as the dancers, a fellow asked her to dance. It was a slow number and he grabbed her tightly. As she tried to stiffen her body in order to push him away, he held her tighter. With the tension he was creating, words refused to come and going around a turn he stood on her toe. She moaned slightly with pain but he never said a word. He moved around on his feet like a machine moving to the music, no words came from his lips. When the music stopped he asked for the next dance. Not sure how to respond, she decided to let him know that she had arranged to meet her friends and he moved quickly away, muttering under his breath some sort of ejaculation.

At this point Bridgie bumped into a well groomed young man as she walked towards the side of the ballroom, trying to move out of the massive crowd at the centre. He seemed friendly and before the music started he asked her for the next dance. He was curious about where she lived or if she often frequented the Cloudland Ballroom. They spoke about their work and the distance she had travelled to the dance. After a night of constant strain it was refreshing to have a conversation with free flowing words. His name was Andy and when he asked Bridgie for the next dance she was delighted; it was like a new night, all the fellows she had met up to now faded from her mind. She had the last three dances with Andy and he offered her a lift home as he had to pass by her house to get to his own townland.

Bridgie had now to make a difficult decision. What would it be like, taking a lift with a stranger. Her pals had got friendly with other fellows and the car she travelled in earlier would be crowded. She spoke with them about Andy and they all agreed that he seemed like a nice fellow. They got into his car and it was already crowded, two of his sisters as well as three young men were packed into the Volkswagen. She was left sitting between Andy and another fellow in the front of the car. She was practically sitting on the hand brake. Despite the strange sensation of taking a lift with a car load of strangers, she still felt as if she knew Andy all her life. In the back of the car tunes of songs were hummed and the words of 'Boolavogue', 'Fr. Murphy' and 'Wooden Heart' rang out in the darkened space of the moving car, as Bridgie gave instructions to Andy on the turns to take in order to get to the lane that led to her home.

Bridgie lived in a two storey house set in from the road in a big field where a narrow path in the centre led to the front door. The drive through the lane took a few minutes longer. It was a very bright night. The moon was high in the sky, lighting up the countryside with a warm glow. She was nervous that her mother might hear her arriving. Her parents' room at the front of the house absorbed all the sounds from outside and she knew her mother never closed an eye until all her brothers and sisters returned home. Bridgie was delighted Andy walked with her along the path as the noise of the car might bring attention to her arrival. Andy put his arm loosely around her waist but half way up the path he suddenly said "I'll go now." Bridgie got such a shock, just as she thought everything was working out well, that she did not know how to respond. She knew she was home but had no idea this man would run off and leave her on the path alone. He said he would be in Rooskey at the Ballroom during the Christmas holidays and if she was there he would see her.

Bridgie got to her front door, found the key - it was hidden in the same place - and opened the door. The kitchen was warm as the range was smouldering. She helped herself to some currant cake and butter as the dancing had made her hungry and her tummy was empty. Her only consolation was to have some food. She washed it down with milk and decided to go to bed but was unable to sleep. It was only four weeks until Christmas and her mind was taken over by Andy and everything he spoke about.

From this time until Christmas Bridgie was unable to free her mind of Andy and she wondered if she would see him again. She prayed she would meet him in Rooskey during her Christmas holidays. As Christmas got nearer she decided to send him a Christmas card. A lot of time was spent wondering what design of card she should purchase. The cards of the Holy Family were over produced. In the town where she worked, lunch hours were spent searching methodically through the many cards on display but nothing appeared suitable. Eventually a card with a verse in the Irish language seemed appropriate as Andy told her he was in the army and she knew they respected the native language. The card was decorated with Celtic designs and snakes entwined in the letters 'Happy Christmas'. Sending it to the Army Headquarters in Athlone, she hoped he was the only Andy McLooney there.

Bridgie decided to write a simple message: 'Happy Christmas, hope you have a nice time and lots of good luck in 1960.'

She never found out if he got the card. Two years later he said hello on the dance floor as he moved around the floor but never danced with her again. Several years later Bridgie heard that Andy was studying for the priesthood. Other than that, she had her memories, especially at Christmas time.

Harmony by Sandra Bell

Photograph taken by Mary Guckian

GARDEN OF REMEMBRANCE

Four swans dominate the garden,
as the flag unfurls
in the morning breeze.
Water moves in wavelets,
and children bounce
on the grey edges of the pool,
their voices competing
with the noisy traffic
from the street outside.
Creeping vine covers
the surrounding walls,
as pensioners relax
on the wooden seats.
I breathe in the Sunday air
of this busy city, watch
droplets cascade on the pool.

SPRINGTIME

Again, it is spring
in the garden outside my flat;
flowers forcing their colours
above ground,
remind me that in nature,
there still remains
a world of mystery

despite
marvellous inventions
space travel
and new technology.

CHERRY BLOSSOMS

I wake in the morning
and find a garden close by,
enclosed with blossoms,
light and fairy like;
some fall on my shoulder,
some touch the ground,
the whole garden alive.
The wonder of each petal
calms my mind, wakes me up.
The continuous swaying
of each branch, petals moving,
their fragility exposed
as they shake, then burst apart.
·Seeds blow in the wind,
leaves make a carpet underneath,
and life is brighter,
full of joy; my body
awakes to this new day.

THE WEIR AT LUCAN

In their coloured anoraks
I see young people canoeing,
swinging their oars as they cut and dip
into the frothy waters.

Around me, daffodil bulbs
shoot stalks out of damp earth,
and falling water clears my head
of office banter and tedious days.

FROSTY MORNING I

Plants stiff with frost,
a solitary rose edged with delicate lace;
the night air has tightened the earth,
prevented birth,
but the sun's heat starts to melt
the shimmering specks away.

All is peaceful on the grass,
the ice is cracking on the river,
ducks swim out
to stretch their feathery bodies,
after a cold night on the river bank.

FROSTY MORNING II

Winter reminds me of wet coats
in the hall and the smoky kitchen heat,
of large logs sizzling,
exerting their wetness on the hearth stone;
cut fresh from the garden,
they fill the flagged floor with warmth.

Each morning pale yellow ashes lie
like floury dust around the fireplace.
A brighter yellow appears in the garden,
across the street,
when the rain beats upon the ash heap.

GRAND CANAL STREET

Among the dirt and overgrown weeds,
pink tinted blossoms cover
the remains of the old hedge,
where residents cared for and trimmed
their gardens over the past century.

Their houses, now lying empty,
wait for the developers
and their long toothed cranes,
to crush to pulp all signs of a way
of life lived on Grand Canal street.

'BALLSBRIDGE WOOD'

I parked my car beneath the trees
that lined the lane behind the library.
Here, I watched the seasons change from
bare branches to full-blown buds, opening
out to shimmering leaves, before they turned
from sombre yellow to burnished bronze.

Now, red bricked houses stand silent
since the developers bored into the earth
with diggers, clearing away brambles, trees
and all the foliage of a thousand years;
no place for blackberries, the fruit I loved
to eat on my lunch-hour feast of air.

FLAGGERS

On Northumberland Road,
in a corner of the garden,
growing tightly together
the icy blue petals on long stalks
are calm,
quietly protecting their roots.

They are taken from damp fields
to where green space is at a premium,
where mews take over large gardens,
and tall trees are cut down,
making way for cement dynasties.

TELESCOPIC GAS HOLDERS

In March
I came to live in Joy Street,
and took a picture
of my house,
and the engineering feat
that crowned the street.

From this place
men came home at sunset,
blackened from the coal
they filled the furnace with,
to make the gas
that ballooned into the crown
each evening,

In July
the cranes move in.
I listened to the scream
and crunch
of contorting rusted metal,
as they crushed
Victorian grandeur
into dust.

Now
my house seems bleak
without the treat
enjoyed each evening,
when patterned sunsets
silently faded
behind the stately
Gasometer.

MADONNA VISION

Fair and fragile she stood on the steps
of the Well Woman Centre,
waiting for the door to open,
her baby weighing heavily in her arms,
her fresh young face looking distracted.

Preoccupied with her troubles,
it was plain for all to see
she seemed alone and lonely,
even with her large baby.
In the circumstances
I had to admire her strength.

COMPUTERS

Computers have taken over
and whose needs are met?
Is it the multinationals?

We make our applications,
fill out the forms,
tick the appropriate boxes,
and allow tedious computers
to make our decisions.

Obeying the questions
on application forms,
we bend our minds
in unoriginal ways,
upsetting our natural rhythms,
to cope with a new age.

PERFUME OF THE SOIL

Sitting on footpaths in Temple Bar,
on pebbled stones at the Royal Hospital,
in bare feet at Lough Derg,
lying on the ground at Fleadhs,
I see young people in black clothes
making contact with the earth.

From carpeted, centrally-heated homes,
and taken to school in buses and cars,
they now yearn for nature
and the smell of the soil.

In the fifties we walked to school,
barefooted along the grass verges
of the stony roads,
and played on the cracked concrete
in the school yard.

We poulticed stone bruises on our feet,
stopped bleeding glass cuts
with cobwebs from the farmyard,
sat on clay ridges guggering
potato slits in spring,
tossed with oat seed as it came out
in torrents from the thresher,
rolled with hay laps in summer months.

We came home in wet clothes
from cycling to the store
and smelled the tweeds drying
on the kitchen hearth,
keeping us in touch
with the earth's crust.

Graffiti at Dublin Docks

Photograph taken by Mary Guckian

GRAFFITI

Young people meander
through dark streets
in the night hours,
and brighten the walls
of grey buildings
with rich colours
from spray cans.

In the beginning
were drawings of animals
in dark caves,
and that hunting spirit,
confined to concrete jungles,
among stifled lives,
releases its energy
in drawings and images,
brightening inner cities
with vibrant decoration
on plain doors,
and the gable walls
of warehouses
in the city's docks,
giving structure to the lives
of Tomo and Gismo.

AGE AND AUTUMN

In their autumn colours,
the trees stand upright,
bringing joy with their turning.
When we are young
we think looks more important
but these soon decay,
and the heart longs for more
than a beautiful surface.
I anticipate all we will learn,
when I observe trees
turning old with grace.

AFTER THE EXHIBITION

On a cold frosty morning
in the hotel lobby,
where the fireplace is full of cinders
and the photographs wait
to be taken off the walls,
the guests in the hallway
smile sleepy sad farewells,
as they collect week-end cases,
and prepare to drive back to the city.
The theatre festival has ended
with many promises
waiting to be fulfilled,
while the created memories
are pushed back, to concentrate
on the five day week ahead.

STANDING STONES

At the highest point
of Ireland's counties,
we walk around
the standing stones,
remembering the burials
of many centuries ago.
The view takes us
across many miles
and we see places
our ancestors chose
for their last resting sites.
I feel the history
of the island overwhelm me
and try to capture
a sense of this time,
as sheep graze
on the rich green land.

CROSSING THE BORDER

Crossing the border for the week-end,
to get away from the security of prying-eyes,
the two young people sat across from us.

Visibly, they became more agitated with
every sentence we uttered, over our
abundant breakfast in the Donegal B&B.

Growing up under British cameras, a lifetime
of radar equipment shining on their homes,
their suffering clearly showed in their eyes.

Afraid to look at us, suspicious of openness,
and terrified of our friendly questions,
for they were reared under searchlights,

and soldiers watched them day after day,
while playing as children. Later surveillance
continued at the factory where they worked.

They found week-ends across the border
opened up a new life, where no one watched
or scrutinised everything they did.

Yet learning to live with this freedom
after a lifetime of intimidation, demanded
adjustment in the hills of Donegal.

Emigrants Cottage

Photograph taken by Mary Guckian

ONE MAN'S RETIREMENT

In Oxford we watched for three months,
the old man, his leg in plaster,
lean against the wall outside the building,
where the Simon people cared for him.

He always gave a friendly greeting,
with his Irish accent, putting some life
back into our tired bodies,
as we rushed by on our way to work.

His younger mates preferred
the benches further down the street,
where they drank the bottle of cider,
hidden away from the night before.

Later in the day, senile old ladies
gathered on benches and listened
to the lilting of his Irish brogue.

AT STROKESTOWN HOUSE

After driving in the dark
through an arch of tall trees,
we parked in the half moon space
shaped by this big house,
and smelled the mulled wine
as it wafted out the door.

On either side of the hallway,
in two large rooms, people admired
the red fires glowing in the old grates,
the walls lined with pieces of Delft,
candlesticks, ornaments, paintings.

Then I remembered
why these artefacts were here,
how tenants were punished
if they did not pay their rent.
A shipload drowned at sea,
after fleeing from the famine years.

In the library, I listened
to thirty two voices from Longford
and Mullingar, singing carols
and bringing the Christmas story to life.
Later, in the kitchen we drank
steaming wine and mince pies.

Leaving the large rooms behind,
in the winding corridor I noticed
how the stones were placed
to make such grand designs.
How men must have slaved
to create all this.

AUTUMN IN OXFORD

Walking into meadows,
we wandered across the

steep bridge and watched
the students rowing.

The narrow boats moved
smoothly under the tall

trees and the oars glided
gracefully on the river,

as the instructor called
out from time to time.

Keeping their movements
in tune with nature, they

floated into the landscape,
and we moved further along

the rich carpet. Crackling
sounds filled our ears,

the burnished leaves fell
gently at our feet as our

time together evaporated.
Years later, memories

stir in the landscape
of our drawn out silence.

FLYING

After the long slow drive
on the wet runway,
we glided into the air
where fields of cotton
enclosed
the movement of the plane.

We bumped onto white,
downy cushions,
floating beyond mundanity,
with the trembling clouds
beneath us,
and the noisy engine forming
a foamy bath,
as we flew across Europe.

Our holiday began
on fragile ground,
anticipating freshness,
away from the tyranny
of the familiar,
where most of our time
is spent.

SYDNEY

Lying on a beach in Sydney,
scorched and sore in the dry heat,
the sand burns my toes.

I wander back to drizzly days in Leitrim,
when I paddled in my wellingtons
in puddles on the farm where I grew up.

Here, rain seldom falls,
and only in quick downpours.
I long for soft days and misty rain,
to moisten my face.

SWISHING OF THE OAT SEED

On the bleak street
not a blade of grass,
only dust
from the lorries,
the cement mixers.

A year later
I see a bud appearing;
by Autumn
this one golden blade
has grown tall.

The sound of a swishing oat seed
cheers me up
in grubby flatland.